Starter Questions

1,000+ Questions to get you started

JESSICA AIKEN-HALL

Copyright © 2022 Jessica Aiken-Hall
First Edition.
All rights reserved. No part of this publication may be reproduced, stored in any retrieval system, or transmitted, in any form or by any means, electronic, mechanical, photocopying, recording or otherwise, without the prior written permission of the author. If you would like permission to use material from the book (other than for review purposes), please contact http://www. jessicaaikenhall.com/contact

Table of Contents

How to Use This Book	4
10 Questions	6
Questions to Get You Started	
• Life Events- Childhood	16
• Life Events- Adulthood	22
Questions for Veterans	39
Questions to Get You Thinking	42
Tough Topics	84
Some of Your Favorite Things	86
What's Next	89
Notes	90

When you lose a loved one, it is often too late to ask to hear that story about (fill in the blank). When you heard about it the first time, you may have been preoccupied and didn't give them your full attention, or you simply forgot. Now that they are gone you can't remember the details. It can be devastating to be left without the answers you are searching for.

None of us are going to live forever, and unfortunately, unless we take time to preserve our stories they are going to leave this world with us.

Between these pages you will find over 1,000 questions that will help you share the significant pieces of your life that you want your loved ones to remember. The questions between these pages will help preserve your legacy.

Life Story Starter Questions is designed to let you skip around and only answer what you want to share. With a mixture of serious and fun questions everyone will find something to write about!

How to Use *Life Story Starter Questions*

- Use the questions to share your story.
- Use the questions to capture a loved one's story.
- Use the questions to get to know a new friend or partner.
- Use the questions to journal.
- The possibilities are endless!

There are many ways to preserve your story.

- Record your voice on a voice recorder
- Record yourself on camera
- Handwrite your answers
- Use photos to go along with your stories
- Journal
- Type out the responses
- Create a blog
- Create a shared drive online and share with loved ones
- Turn your work into a book that can be shared with family and friends
- Publish your stories to share with the world

Are you ready to get started?!?

Why is sharing your story important to you? What are you hoping happens to the memories you share? Who do you hope reads it?

What is your definition of success?

When have you had your greatest successes? What did you learn from this? What advice or suggestions do you have for others?

What is your definition of failure?

When have you had your greatest failure? What did you learn from this? What advice or suggestions do you have for others?

If you could have designed your life knowing what you know now, what would it look like? What changes would you make? What would you keep the same?

If you were able to spend one more day with a loved one that has passed away, what would you do or talk about?

What do you love most about life?

Choose one of your earliest memories and write about the event. Describe everything you can remember, including who was with you, what happened, your feelings, sounds, and smells.

If someone were to ask you what your most important life lessons have been, what would you say? Why?

What objects tells the story of your life?

Who is the most important person in your life? Describe the reasons why.

Questions to Get You Started

Life Events – Childhood

- What year were you born? On what date? What day of the week was it?
- Did your parents tell you anything about the day you were born?
- Where were you born?
- Why were you given the first (and middle) name(s) that you have?
- What's your first, most vivid memory?
- What was the apartment or house like that you grew up in?
- How many bedrooms did it have? Bathrooms?
- What was your bedroom like?
- Can you describe the neighborhood you grew up in?
- What's something you want to share about your parents?
- Where were they born?
- When were they born?
- What memories do you have of them?
- Who was stricter: your mother or your father?
- Do you have a vivid memory of something you did that you were disciplined for?

- Did your parents have a good marriage?
- How did your family earn money? How did your family compare to others in the neighborhood – richer, poorer, the same?
- What kinds of things did your family spend money on?
- How many brothers and sisters do you have?
- When were they born?
- What memories do you have of each of them from when you were growing up?
- Did you have grandparents?
- Where were they born?
- When were they born?
- What do you remember about them?
- When did they die?
- Did you have any pets?
- What were you like as a child?
- What did you like to eat?
- What did you do for fun?
- What were your favorite toys or games?
- Did you have a secret place or a favorite hiding spot?
- What kinds of clothing did you wear?
- Did you get an allowance? How much?
- Did you spend it right away, or save it?

- What did you buy?
- What responsibilities did you have at home when you were young?
- What kind of school did you go to?
- Were you a good student?
- What was your favorite subject? Least favorite?
- Who were your friends?
- Who was your favorite teacher and why?
- Did you have any heroes or role models when you were a child?
- How did you spend your summer holidays?
- What were your favorite summer activities?
- Where did your family go on vacations?
- How did your family celebrate holidays (e.g. Thanksgiving, Christmas, New Year, Easter, Memorial Day)? Did lots of relatives get together? What food was served?
- What traditions did you have year after year?
- What was the best gift you remember receiving as a child?
- What did you want to be when you grew up?
- What big world events do you remember from the time you were growing up?

- What's different about growing up today from when you were growing up?
- When you were a teenager, what did you do for fun?
- Did you have a favorite spot to "hang out"?
- What time did you have to be home at night?
- Did you ever get into any trouble?
- Were there any phrases that were popular when you were a teenager?
- What did you like to wear?
- How did your parents feel about the way you talked and what you wore?
- When did you learn how to drive?
- Who taught you?
- What was your first car like?
- What was your graduation from high school like?
- What dreams and goals did you have for your life when you graduated?
- What were your family's attitudes towards alcohol, smoking, and drugs?
- What was the discipline like at home? ¬
- What sorts of things were your parents strict about? How? Why?
- What did you do in your spare time? (clubs/youth organizations /cinema/theatre?)

- Did you stick to a group of friends?
- Did your parents expect to meet your friends?
- Did your parents disapprove of any of your activities? If so, why?
- How did you feel about moving away from home?
- Did you keep in touch with your family? How? Why?
- What story do you remember most about your childhood?
- Are there any happy, sad, or instructive lessons you learned while growing up?
- Did your parents name you after anyone?
- Did your birth take place in a hospital, at home? Was there a doctor or midwife present?
- Do you have any special memories of your grandparents?
- What important life lessons did you learn from your parents?
- What family stories or memories were passed down to you from your parents or grandparents?
- Describe a person or situation from your childhood that had a profound effect on the way you look at life.
- What thing(s) did you mother/father always say?
- What manners were you taught? Are they still important to you?

- Did you have any imaginary friends? When did you notice them and how long were they part of your life?
- Did you grow up on a farm? What kind of animals were on the farm?
- What stories have you been told about your birth?
- Did you have a favorite stuffed animal or toy? Did it have a name? Describe what it looked like and how it made you feel.
- Did you like your name? Have you ever wished it were different?
- What inventions do you most remember?

Life Events – Adulthood

- Did you go to university or college?
- What made you choose the college you went to?
- How did you decide what you wanted to study?
- How did you decide what you wanted to do with your life? How do you feel about that choice?
- What's the most memorable family vacation you took?
- What was your first job? What did you like or not like about it?
- What job did you do most of your life? What did you like most about it? Least?
- What job would you never do no matter how much it paid?
- What did you want to be when you were younger?
- Is there one job you'd never ever do?
- What did you want to be when you grew up?
- What do you remember most about your first job?
- How old were you when you started working?
- Would you rather make more money doing a job you hate or less doing one you love?
- What's the worst job you've ever had?
- What originally got you interested in the work you did?
- What's the best career decision you've ever made?
- What's the worst career decision you've ever made?

- What career advice would you give to your younger self?
- How do you separate your work life from your home life?
- Are you looking forward to retiring, or do you plan to work as long as possible?
- Have you ever had "imposter syndrome"?
- What do you think about workaholics?
- What qualities do you look for in a boss?
- What energizes you about your career?
- What's the best career advice you've ever heard?
- What job would you never do no matter how much it paid?
- What's the worst career advice you've ever received?
- Who has had the biggest impact on your career choice?
- If you could do it all over again, would you pursue the same career? Why or why not?
- How did you meet your spouse? What did you like about him/her?
- How and when did you get engaged?
- When did you get married? How old were you?
- Where did you get married?
- What was your wedding like?
- What makes your spouse special or unique?

- What was the first big purchase you made with your spouse?
- How many children do you have? When were they born?
- How did you decide what to name each?
- What is something funny or embarrassing one of your children said at an early age that you'll never forget?
- What do you remember about holiday celebrations?
- Is there one holiday memory that stands out for you?
- How did you feel about raising your children?
- What was the best part? The hardest part?
- What makes you proud of your children?
- How is your father/mother like you? Unlike you?
- What do you remember about the birth of your children?
- What is the best thing about being a parent?
- What is the best thing about being a grandparent?
- Do you know the meaning of your family name?
- Are there stories about the origins of your family name?
- Have you ever had any nicknames as a child or as an adult? Where did they come from?
- How are you like your mother? Unlike her?

- How are you like your father? Unlike him?
- What was most important to your parents?
- Do you feel you're like any of your grandparents? In what ways?
- How are your children like you? Unlike you?
- What do you think are your three best qualities? Your three worst?
- Which do you think you have the most of: talent, intelligence, education, or persistence? How has it helped you in your life?
- Do you have any special sayings or expressions?
- Who are three people in history you admire most and why?
- What have been the three biggest news events during your lifetime and why?
- If you could travel into the future, would you rather see something that specifically relates to you, or something that relates to the future of the country in general? Why?
- If you could have three wishes, what would they be?
- If you won $1 million tomorrow, what would you do with the money?
- What's the highest honor or award you've ever received?

- What's the most memorable phone call you've ever received?
- What's the best compliment you ever received?
- What kinds of things bring you the most pleasure now?
- What kinds of things bring you the most pleasure when you were a younger adult?
- What kinds of things bring you the most pleasure when you were a child?
- What things frighten you now?
- What frightened you when you were a younger adult?
- What frightened you when you were a child?
- What's the one thing you've always wanted but still don't have?
- Do you feel differently about yourself now from how you felt when you were younger? How?
- What do you think has stayed the same about you throughout life? What do you think has changed?
- Do you have any hobbies or special interests?
- Do you enjoy any particular sports?
- What's your typical day like now? How is it different from your daily routines in the past?
- Is the present better or worse than when you were younger?

- What do you do for fun?
- Who do you trust and depend on?
- What things are most important to you now? Why?
- How have your dreams and goals changed through your life?
- What do you see when you look in the mirror?
- What do you remember about your 20s?
- What do you remember about your 30s?
- What do you remember about your 40s?
- What do you remember about your 50s?
- What do you remember about your 60s?
- What events stand out in your mind?
- How was each age different from the one before it?
- What birthday were you least enthusiastic about? Why?
- If you could go back to any age, which age would it be and why?
- How do you feel now about growing old?
- What's the hardest thing about growing older?
- What's the best thing about growing older?
- What were your parents like when they got older?
- Did you have any expectations at points in your life about what growing older would be like for you?

- Is there anything you wish you'd done differently?
- Do you think about the future and make plans?
- What are your concerns for the future?
- If you live another 20-30 years, what will you do?
- Do you want to live another 20-30 years?
- What do you look forward to now?
- What's your most cherished family tradition? Why is it important?
- What have you liked best about your life so far?
- What's your happiest or proudest moment?
- What do you feel have been the important successes in your life?
- What have been the biggest frustrations in you life?
- What's the most difficult thing that ever happened to you? How did you deal with it?
- What do you think the turning points have been in your life?
- Are there times of your life that you remember more vividly than others? Why?
- What have been the most influential experiences in your life?
- If you were writing the story of your life, how would you divide it into chapters?

- What, if anything, would you have done differently in your life?
- What do you know now that you wish you'd known when you were young?
- What have you thrown away in your life that you wish you hadn't?
- What have you held on to that's important and why is it important?
- What "junk" have you held on to and why?
- Over time, how have you changed the way you look at life/people?
- What advice did your grandparents or parents give you that you remember best?
- Do you have a philosophy of life?
- What's your best piece of advice for living?
- If a young person came to you asking "what's the most important thing for living a good life?" what would you tell them?
- How do you define a "good life" or a "successful life"?
- Do you think a person needs to first overcome serious setbacks or challenges to be truly successful?
- In what way is it important to know your limitations in your life or career?

- If you had the power to solve one and only one problem in the world, what would it be and why?
- What do you see as your place or purpose in life? How did you come to that conclusion?
- What would you like your children and grandchildren to remember about you?
- If you could write a message to each of your children and grandchildren and put it in a time capsule for them to read 20 years from now, what would you write to each?
- What's the funniest family story you remember?
- Do you follow any religious traditions? If so, which one, and what is it like?
- Have you ever changed faiths?
- What role do your beliefs play in your life today?
- What were the most joyous, fulfilling times of your life?
- If you could do one thing differently in your life, what would it be?
- What have you learned over your lifetime that you'd like to share with the younger generation?
- What would you consider to be the most important inventions during your lifetime?

- What is the most beautiful place you have ever visited and what was it like?
- What is the longest trip you have ever gone on? Where did you go?
- What is the favorite place you ever visited and what was it like?
- What person had the most positive influence on your life? What did he or she do to influence you?
- Is there a person that really changed the course of your life by something that he or she did? How did it happen?
- Do you remember someone saying something to you that had a big impact on how you lived your life? Who said it, and what did that person say?
- What about special holiday traditions or recipes passed on to you?
- Are there any special family heirlooms that were handed down to you?
- What kinds of foods did you eat often?
- Where did your food come from? A grocery store, a nearby farm, your family's farm/garden?
- Did you have any animals or pets growing up? Which was your favorite?

- Was your family religious? What place of worship did you attend?
- Do you remember what it was like finding out you would soon be a parent?
- What were your children's births like? At the hospital, at home? Who was there?
- Did you move around much? Why did you move and to where?
- What was your favorite way to spend time with your kids?
- What was the hardest part of raising kids? The best part?
- What kind of music did you like to listen to?
- What kind of books/magazines did you like to read?
- When did you get your driver's license?
- When did you get your first car? What was it?
- What did you like most about your childhood?
- When you misbehaved, what was your punishment?
- Did you marry? If not why did you chose to remain single?
- Did you marry for love or another reason?
- What was your wedding like?
- Where did you get married? Where was your honeymoon?

- Where did you live when newly married?
- How do your children's lives differ from yours?
- What were your children like as kids?
- What were they like as teenagers?
- When your kids misbehaved, how did you punish them?
- When they excelled how did you reward them?
- Why did you chose to live where you did?
- What were the happiest days that you remember?
- What were your proudest accomplishments?
- What do you recall as the time you felt most proud of each of your children? Why?
- Do you have any grandchildren or great-grandchildren and where do they live?
- Who did you first fall in love with?
- How and where did you meet?
- What did you talk about?
- Do you remember a special present you bought or received from him/her?
- Did you have a favorite place to go together?
- Do you have a special memory of a time you spent with that person?
- Are you still together or, if not, why did you part?

- If you could go back and re-live any part of my life, what it would be?
- What was your proudest moment?
- What main things guided your life decisions?
- At times of stress in your life, what got you through it?
- What was your greatest fear growing up? How did you dealt with it?
- What is the most important lessons you have learned?
- Who was the one person you admired most? Why?
- What are you most sorry about?
- What cause were you most concerned with?
- What was the hardest thing you ever had to do?
- What/Who was the greatest influence in your life?
- What movie or book impacted the way you lived your life? Why?
- What is your most treasured possession and why?
- As you look back, what are the three most fantastic changes you witnessed?
- What are some of the principles that you have lived by? What guides you?
- How well have you been able to live by those principles?
- Describe your spiritual or religious beliefs.

- What were your grandparents' and parents' beliefs?
- Do you still practice the faith you were born into? If not, when and why did you change?
- Have you participated in any celebrations with your faith? If so, what were they, and how old were you?
- Have you done any work with youth groups?
- Have you traveled to spread your faith to other people?
- Write about a memorable experience from that time.
- How has your faith helped to guide you through life?
- Was there a special time in your life when your faith sustained you in a time of crisis?
- What is your favorite Scripture and why?
- Share a story about a prayer that was answered.
- Do you believe in miracles? Have you experience one?
- Describe some of the ways that your life has been blessed by your faith.
- What would you like to share in regard to your faith?
- How much time do you spend with your family?
- How would you describe your relationship with your mother?
- What qualities do you admire about your parents?
- What was your father or mother like at home? How did he or she act different outside of family?

- Which parent are you closer to and why?
- Which family member makes the best food?
- How has your opinion of your family changed over the years?
- If you're close with your family, what's the hardest part about spending time away from them?
- Do you wish you had a bigger family, or are you happy with its current size?
- Which family member has had the greatest impact on you?
- What does your family's last name mean?
- Who's the best gift-giver in your family?
- What's your favorite story about your grandparents?
- Have you ever mapped out your family tree?
- Were you close with your family growing up?
- How do you define your family now?
- What traits are most important to you in your family members?
- Who in your family makes you feel the safest?
- Have you ever been to a family reunion?
- If you could change your relationship with a family member, would you? If so, with whom?
- What do you admire most about your mother and father?

- What was it like growing up as the youngest/oldest/middle/only child?
- Does your family ever take trips together?
- What's your favorite family memory?
- What TV family most reminds you of your own?
- Do you ever wish you were raised differently?
- What's the best piece of advice a family member has given you?
- Do you wish you had more siblings? If so, why?
- Did you ever hide anything from or lie to your parents?
- If you had a family business, what would it be?
- Do you and your family have any nicknames for each other?
- What's your favorite way to spend time with your family?
- How do you show your family you love them?
- What's your favorite family tradition?
- What's the most important holiday you spend with your family and why?
- Who in your family would you describe as a "character"?
- How do you feel about family events?
- What's something your family would be surprised to learn about you?

- Which family member do you confide in most?
- How do you deal with arguments between family members?
- What is the most enjoyable thing your family has done together in the last three years?
- What's more important: family or friends?
- Do you have any friends you would consider family?
- Did you ever get to meet your great-grandparents?
- What personality traits do you share with your relatives?
- What physical traits do you share with your relatives?
- What stories did your family members tell you growing up?
- How did your parents (and/or grandparents) meet?
- What makes you proud of your family?
- Who's the newest member of your family?
- What can always bring your family together?
- Who taught you how to drive?
- Have you ever ridden or driven a motorcycle?
- What awards, honors, medals or prizes have you won?
- What traits run in your family?
- If you were adopted, have you tried to find your biological family?

Questions for Veterans

- Were you drafted or did you enlist?
- Where were you living at the time?
- If you joined, what was your motivation?
- Why did you pick the service branch you joined?
- Do you recall your first days in service? What did it feel like?
- Talk about your boot camp/training experiences. What do you remember about your instructors?
- How did you get through it?
- Which war (s) did you serve in?
- Where exactly did you go?
- Do you remember your arrival and what it was like?
- What was your job/assignment?
- Did you see combat?
- Were there any casualties in your unit?
- Talk about a couple of your most memorable experiences.
- Were you a prisoner of war? If so, talk about your experiences and when freed.
- Were you awarded any medals or citations? What did you do to earn them?
- What was the food like?

- How did you stay in touch with your family?
- Did you have enough supplies?
- Did you feel pressure or stress?
- Was there something special you did for good luck?
- How did people entertain themselves?
- Were there entertainers?
- What did you do when on leave?
- Where did you traveled while in the service?
- Do you recall any particularly humorous or unusual events?
- Did you and others pull pranks? If so, describe some.
- Do you have photographs? Who is in them?
- What did you think of officers or fellow soldiers?
- Did you keep a personal diary?
- Do you recall the day your service ended? How did you feel? Where were you?
- What did you do in the days and weeks that followed?
- Did you work or go back to school?
- Was your education supported by the GI Bill?
- Did you make any close friendships while in the service?
- Did you continue any of those friendships? For how long?

- Did you join a veteran's organization?
- What did you go on to do as a career after your service?
- Did your military experience influence your thinking about war or about the military in general?
- If you are in a veteran's organization, what kind of activities does your post or association have?
- Do you attend reunions?
- How did your service and experiences affect your life?
- Is there anything you would like to add about your time in the service?

Questions to Get You Thinking

- What's your philosophy in life?
- What's the one thing you would like to change about yourself?
- Are you religious or spiritual?
- Do you consider yourself an introvert or an extrovert?
- What was the best phase in your life?
- What was the worst phase in your life?
- What makes you feel accomplished?
- Who is that one person you can talk to about just anything?
- Have you ever lost someone close to you?
- If you are in a bad mood, do you prefer to be left alone or have someone to cheer you up?
- What's an ideal weekend for you?
- Do you judge a book by its cover?
- Are you confrontational?
- Did you ever write a journal?
- What are you most thankful for?
- Do you believe in second chances?
- What's the one thing that people always misunderstand about you?
- What is your idea of a perfect vacation?

- What's on your bucket list? Have you crossed anything off of it?
- When have you felt your biggest adrenaline rush?
- What is the craziest thing you've ever done and would you do it again?
- If a genie granted you 3 wishes right now, what would you wish for?
- What's your biggest regret in life?
- What do you think about when you're by yourself?
- What's been your biggest mistake so far in life and what did you learn from it?
- How would you describe your best friend?
- What's something you can't go a day without doing?
- What's the most spontaneous thing you've done?
- What's the craziest thing you've ever done for love?
- What's your biggest pet peeve?
- What accomplishment are you most proud of?
- What is one dream you have yet to accomplish?
- What is your greatest fear?
- What are three things you value most about a person?
- Who are five people you are closest with?
- What is the greatest struggle you've overcome?
- If you could live anywhere in the world where would it be?

- What's the most exciting thing that's happened to you?
- What's one thing that bothers you most about the world today?
- If you could change one thing about yourself what would it be?
- If you could change one thing about the world what would it be?
- What is the weirdest thing about you?
- What would the people closest to you say is your best quality?
- If you could tell your former self one thing right now what would it be?
- What food could you not live without?
- What's closest you've ever come to being arrested?
- What was your best birthday?
- What's one thing you wish you knew how to do?
- Where's one place you'd like to go that you haven't been?
- What was the last book you read? And When?
- Where do you usually get your news?
- What would you consider your greatest accomplishment so far?
- If you could get away with anything what would you do?

- Who is your greatest hero?
- What's the greatest risk you've ever taken?
- Why are we here?
- If heaven is real and you died tomorrow, would you get in?
- Do you believe in fate?
- How do you think people see you?
- If you had the ability to erase something that you did in the past, what would it be?
- What song makes you unconditionally happy?
- If you could have anybody else's life, who's would you take?
- What fictional character do you most relate to?
- At age 5 what did you want to be when you grew up?
- If you could go anywhere in the world right now, where would you go?
- What is your biggest regret?
- If you died tomorrow, what would you wish you had done?
- Can you pin point the moment in your life where you were the happiest?
- What song makes you unconditionally sad?
- If past lives are real, what was yours?

- What is your biggest accomplishment?
- If you could do one thing without suffering the consequences, what would you do?
- What is the strangest dream you've ever had?
- What is the darkest thought you've ever had?
- What is the darkest thing you've never told anybody?
- Is there something out there, a thought, an idea, a current event, or a fear that you find deeply unsettling?
- What would you consider to be your deepest fear?
- Is there an activity that calms you? A place or a thing that makes you feel at ease?
- What do you do or where do you go when you need to be alone?
- What makes you feel like you need to be alone?
- Can you remember a time in your life you felt the most alive? Write everything about that memory.
- When have you felt the lowest in your life?
- Where have you felt the most failure?
- Where have you felt the most success?
- Write about the facts or harsh truths you choose to ignore but know you shouldn't.
- Where do you find meaning in your life?
- What makes you feel uneasy? Overwhelmed? Anxious?

- When have you felt like you were living life to the fullest? When have you felt like you weren't?
- What is the first lie you ever told? Which is the biggest?
- What is the first secret you ever kept from anybody? Which is the biggest?
- Are you a religious or spiritual person? Write about why and how.
- Have you always had the same political beliefs? Is there something that impacted them?
- Have you ever been in love? Write about the times you have been.
- Write about the times someone broke your heart.
- Why did you cry the last time you did so?
- Have you ever cried tears of joy?
- What did you do when you hurt someone the most?
- If your life was a movie or a book what would be the title to it?
- When have you caused the most harm to yourself?
- What has been the biggest change you ever made that made you the most proud of yourself?
- Think about the people you love the most in your life, what do you do for them?

- Is home for you a place or a feeling? Describe that place or describe that feeling.
- If you could be anywhere other than where you are right now, where would you be and what would you be looking at?
- Have you ever questioned your sanity and why?
- What is your most cherished childhood memory?
- Have you ever had dreams about a past life?
- Do you have any recurring dreams or nightmares?
- Do you believe more in fate or that we are the creators of our own destinies because we are governed by free will?
- Do you believe in extraterrestrial life? Elaborate on why or why not.
- Would you find more comfort in the theoretical idea that that we were the most advanced species in outer space or would you find more comfort in the idea that we weren't?
- What would be your thought process if you were presented with irrefutable evidence that a god didn't exist? What would be your thought process if you were presented with irrefutable evidence that a god did exist?

- What do you think was there before the universe came into creation?
- Do you believe in other dimensions and parallel universes?
- How do you define art?
- If you could have the option of eliminating pain from your life would you choose to do so? Why or why not?
- Is a life exclusive to pleasure (no suffering) worthwhile?
- What do you think happens after death, if anything?
- If you could be given the date of your death would you want to know it?
- Presented with the opportunity to be immortal would you take it?
- Would you rather be loved or love?
- How do you define beauty?
- Where does happiness come from? Define what happiness means to you.
- Do you believe yourself to be truly free? If so, why? If not, what is holding you back?
- Deja-vu: is there anything to it or merely coincidence?
- If you were given a choice to choose your manner of death, how would you die?

- If you could have any animal in the world as a pet, what would it be and why?
- If you were given a chance to explore the oceans, go to outer space or visit 50 different countries, which one you choose and why?
- Out of the negative emotions of greed, anger, jealousy and hate, which one would you say affects you the most? Explain.
- Out of the positive emotions of compassion, positivity, enthusiasm and initiative, which one is your biggest strength? Explain.
- If you could be President of your country for an hour, what is the one thing that you would change?
- Has another's pain ever given you joy? Be totally honest.
- What is your biggest supernatural or paranormal fear?
- If you were forced to pick one religion on this planet, which one would it be and why?
- What is the most romantic and loving thing you have ever done for somebody?
- What is the most adventurous thing you have ever done in your life?
- What's your day-to-day mantra?

- What quote resonates with you more than any other?
- What trait do you envy in others?
- What skill do you wish you had?
- How do you wish to be remembered?
- How would you summarize your life purpose?
- What was the best vacation you ever took and why?
- What are your hobbies, and how did you get into them?
- What was your favorite age growing up?
- What was the last thing you read?
- Would you say you're more of an extrovert or an introvert?
- What was the last TV show you binge-watched?
- Favorites Do you have a favorite holiday? Why or why not?
- If you could only eat one food for the rest of your life, what would it be?
- What's your go-to guilty pleasure?
- In the summer, would you rather go to the beach or go camping?
- How old were you when you had your first celebrity crush, and who was it?
- What's one thing that can instantly make your day better?

- What song always gets you out on the dance floor?
- What activity instantly calms you?
- Ideally, how would you spend your birthday?
- What's the best joke you've ever heard?
- Would you rather cook or order in?
- What's your most prized possession and why?
- Is there any product that you couldn't live without?
- If you could have any exotic animal as a pet, which would it be?
- What would be the first thing you'd do if you won the lottery?
- What's your favorite way to unwind?
- How do you enjoy spending your alone time?
- What causes are you passionate about?
- What's something you're excited about right now?
- What's an essential part of your daily routine?
- What's the best gift you've ever received?
- What's the worst gift you've ever received, and what did you do about it?
- What annoys you most?
- Who do you most like spending time with and why?
- What do you think makes someone a "good person"?

- Do you believe in love at first sight?
- How do you show kindness to others?
- Do you believe in soulmates? Why or why not?
- What do you look for in a friendship?
- How do your daily priorities reflect your overall values in life?
- Do you believe time you enjoy wasting is not wasted time?
- What life lessons have you had to learn the hard way?
- Do you believe what is meant for you will never miss you?
- Have you ever experienced true love, and how did you know?
- What's a relationship deal breaker for you?
- If you had only one sense (hearing, touch, sight, etc.), which would you want?
- Do you volunteer at all?
- What makes you feel at peace?
- What are you most proud of in your life?
- What makes you feel most accomplished?
- Who do you admire most in the world?
- Which of your personality traits are you most proud of?

- What's the first thing you look for in a partner and/or friend?
- How has your perspective on the world changed over time?
- Do you live by any piece of advice or motto?
- How can someone earn your trust?
- How can someone lose your trust?
- Would you rather someone be honest and hurt your feelings or lie to protect them?
- If you could snap your fingers and instantly make the world better, what would you do?
- Do you believe in astrology? Why or why not?
- Have you ever lost a friend? If so, what happened?
- Family If you could only teach one thing to your child, what would it be?
- What's the scariest thing you've ever done, and why did you do it?
- Where do you get your news?
- What is your biggest irrational fear?
- What is your definition of success?
- Are you an organ donor, and how did you come to that decision?
- Do you believe you should do one thing a day that scares you?

- What line should someone never cross with you?
- How do you define beauty?
- How do you interact with someone who disagrees with you?
- Do you think our dreams have hidden meanings?
- When you want to give up, what keeps you going?
- Do you live by any words of wisdom?
- What's the first step you take in trying to achieve a new goal?
- How do you turn a "no" into a "yes"?
- What do you do to overcome a personal setback?
- Is it easy for you to accept help in achieving your dreams?
- If you could do anything, besides what you're doing now, what would you do?
- What do you regret not doing?
- If you had unlimited money to start your own business, what would it be?
- If you found out today was your last day on Earth, what would you do?
- If you could live anywhere in the world, where would it be?
- If you could relive one moment in your life, which would it be?

- Which famous person in history would you want to spend the day with?
- If you could time travel, when and where would you go?
- Do you think you'll likely accomplish all your dreams?
- If you could magically become famous, would you want to?
- Do you believe in ghosts—why or why not? If so, are you afraid of ghosts?
- Do you have any special skills?
- Can you write in cursive?
- If you could live in a movie, which one would it be and why?
- If you could have a super power, what would it be?
- If you could go back to anytime in history, where would you go?
- If you came back in your next life as an animal, what animal would you be?
- What's the first thing you do in the morning?
- What's the last thing you do at night?
- What's the most unusual place you've fallen asleep?
- At a party, where can someone find you?
- Who would play you in the movie of your life?

- Do you trust your own memory? Why or why not?
- Which fictional character do you relate to most?
- When was the last time you cried and why?
- What's your most controversial opinion about something mundane?
- What was your all-time favorite Halloween costume?
- What's the weirdest thing you do when you're alone?
- What's the silliest argument you've ever been in?
- What's the worst argument you've ever been in?
- What's the most ridiculous outfit you've ever worn?
- If you could own a mythical creature (unicorn, phoenix, etc.), which one would you pick?
- What's your favorite story about yourself?
- If you could change anything about yourself, would you? If so, what and why?
- When was the last time you tried something new?
- What's the most sensible thing you've ever heard someone say?
- What gets you excited about life?
- What life lesson did you learn the hard way?
- What do you wish you spent more time doing five years ago?
- Do you ask enough questions or do you settle for what you know?

- Who do you love and what are you doing about it?
- What's a belief that you hold with which many people disagree?
- What can you do today that you were not capable of a year ago?
- Do you think crying is a sign of weakness or strength?
- What would you do differently if you knew nobody would judge you?
- Do you celebrate the things you do have?
- What is the difference between living and existing?
- If not now, then when?
- Have you done anything lately worth remembering?
- What does your joy look like today?
- Is it possible to lie without saying a word?
- If you had a friend who spoke to you in the same way that you sometimes speak to yourself, how long would you allow this person to be your friend?
- Which activities make you lose track of time?
- If you had to teach something, what would you teach?
- What would you regret not fully doing, being or having in your life?
- Are you holding onto something that you need to let go of?

- When you are 80-years-old, what will matter to you the most?
- Life When is it time to stop calculating risk and rewards and just do what you know is right?
- How old would you be if you didn't know how old you are?
- Would you break the law to save a loved one?
- What makes you smile?
- When it's all said and done, will you have said more than you've done?
- If you had the opportunity to get a message across to a large group of people, what would your message be?
- If the average human lifespan was 40 years, how would you live your life differently?
- What do we all have in common besides our genes that makes us human?
- If you could choose one book as a mandatory read for all high school students, which book would you choose?
- What is important enough to go to war over?
- Which is worse, failing or never trying?
- When was the last time you listened to the sound of your own breathing?

- What's something you know you do differently than most people?
- If you could instill one piece of advice in a newborn baby's mind, what advice would you give?
- What is the most desirable trait another person can possess?
- What are you most grateful for?
- Is stealing to feed a starving child wrong?
- What do you want most?
- Are you more worried about doing things right, or doing the right things?
- What has life taught you recently?
- What is the one thing you would most like to change about the world?
- Where do you find inspiration?
- Can you describe your life in a six word sentence?
- If we learn from our mistakes, why are we always so afraid to make a mistake?
- What impact do you want to leave on the world?
- What is the most defining moment of your life thus far?
- In the haste of your daily life, what are you not seeing?
- What lifts your spirits when life gets you down?

- Have you ever regretted something you didn't say or do?
- Has your greatest fear ever come true?
- Why do we think of others the most when they're gone?
- What is your most beloved childhood memory?
- Is it more important to love or be loved?
- If you had the chance to go back in time and change one thing would you do it?
- If a doctor gave you five years to live, what would you try to accomplish?
- What is the difference between falling in love and being in love?
- Who do you think stands between you and happiness?
- What is the difference between innocence and ignorance?
- What is the simplest truth you can express in words?
- Can there be happiness without sadness?
- Can there be pleasure without pain?
- Can there be peace without war?
- What's the one thing you'd like others to remember about you at the end of your life?
- Is there such a thing as perfect?

- To what degree have you actually controlled the course your life has taken?
- Life What does it mean to be human?
- If you looked into the heart of your enemy, what do you think you would find that is different from what is in your own heart?
- What do you love most about yourself?
- Where would you most like to go and why?
- What small act of kindness were you once shown that you will never forget?
- Life What is your happiest childhood memory? What makes it so special?
- Do you own your things or do your things own you?
- Would you rather lose all of your old memories or never be able to make new ones?
- How do you deal with someone in a position of power who wants you to fail?
- Life What do you have that you cannot live without?
- When you close your eyes what do you see?
- What sustains you on a daily basis?
- What are your top five personal values?
- What personal prisons have you built out of fears?
- What one thing have you not done that you really want to do?

- What three words would you use to describe the last three months of your life?
- Is it ever right to do the wrong thing?
- Is it ever wrong to do the right thing?
- How would you describe 'freedom' in your own words?
- If you could ask one person, alive or dead, only one question, who would you ask and what would you ask?
- If happiness was the national currency, what kind of work would make you rich?
- What is your number one goal for the next six months?
- Would you ever give up your life to save someone else?
- What is the meaning of 'peace' to you?
- What are three moral rules you will never break?
- What does it mean to allow another person to truly love you?
- Who or what do you think of when you think of love?
- If your life was a novel, what would be the title and how would your story end?
- What would you not give up for $1,000,000 in cash?
- When do you feel most like yourself?
- What is your greatest challenge?

- How do you know when it's time to continue holding on or time to let go?
- How do you define success?
- If someone could tell you the exact day and time you are going to die, would you want them to tell you?
- If you could live one day of your life over again, what day would you choose?
- What can money not buy?
- If you left this life tomorrow, how would you be remembered?
- Beyond the titles that others have given you, who are you?
- If you could live the next 24 hours and then erase it and start over just once, what would you do?
- Is it possible to know the truth without challenging it first?
- What do you owe yourself?
- Can you think of a time when impossible became possible?
- Why do you matter?
- How have you changed in the last five years?
- What are you sure of in your life?
- When you think of 'home,' what, specifically, do you think of?

- What's the difference between settling for things and accepting the way things are?
- What's your definition of heaven?
- What is your most prized possession?
- What stands between you and happiness?
- What makes a person beautiful?
- Is there ever a time when giving up makes sense?
- Where do you find peace?
- Is it better to have loved and lost or to have never loved at all?
- Who do you trust and why?
- If you were forced to eliminate every physical possession from your life with the exception of what could fit into a single backpack, what would you put in it?
- When does silence convey more meaning than words?
- How do you spend the majority of your free time?
- Who do you think of first when you think of success?
- How will today matter in five years from now?
- How have you helped someone else recently?
- How has someone helped you recently?
- What is your greatest skill?
- What's the next big step you need to take?

- If you knew you were going to die, how would you want to spend your last day?
- If today was the last day of your life, who would you call and what would you tell them?
- Who do you dream about?
- What do you have trouble seeing clearly in your mind?
-
- If you knew you were going to die, how would you want to spend your last day?
- If today was the last day of your life, who would you call and what would you tell them?
- Who do you dream about?
- What do you have trouble seeing clearly in your mind?
- What are you looking forward to?
- What is the number one thing you want to accomplish before you die?
- When is love a weakness?
- What has been the most terrifying moment of your life thus far?
- Who is the strongest person you know?
- If you could take a single photograph of your life, what would it look like?
- What makes today worth living?

- What have you done in the last year that makes you proud?
- What did you learn recently that changed the way you live?
- What is your fondest memory?
- What are the primary components of a happy life?
- How would the world be different if you were never born?
- What are your top three priorities?
- What is the nicest thing someone has ever done for you?
- What do you see when you look into the future?
- What makes you angry? Why?
- What is the most valuable life lesson you learned from your parents?
- What does love feel like?
- What are your favorite simple pleasures?
- If you could go back in time and tell a younger version of yourself one thing, what would you tell?
- What will you never do?
- Excluding romantic relationships, who do you love?
- What is your earliest childhood memory?
- What book has had the greatest influence on your life?

- What was the first accident you were involved in?
- Who was the first famous person you met?
- What was the first trip you remember taking?
- What was your first car?
- What was the first loss you experienced?
- Who was your first friend?
- When was your first time you saw the ocean?
- What was the first election you voted in?
- What was the first concert you went to?
- Did you buy lottery tickets? Is there anyone that you know who have won the lottery?
- List the collections you have had. How old were you when you started each collection? How did each collection start?
- Have you ever been arrested? What happened and what was the outcome?
- Have you ever been the victim of a crime? What was the nature of the crime? Was the perpetrator caught? What was the outcome?
- What are the biggest blocks in your life to real happiness?
- If you had the chance to trade places with another person, who would it be? Why?

- What three questions do you wish you knew the answers to?
- What is the greatest peer pressure you've ever felt?
- What's the biggest lie you once believed was true?
- In your lifetime, what have you done that hurt someone else?
- What's been on your mind most lately?
- What do you think is worth waiting for?
- What chances do you wish you had taken?
- Where else would you like to live? Why?
- What motivates you to get up each day?
- What do you wish you had done differently?
- When was the last time you lied? What did you lie about?
- What made you smile this week?
- What do you do with the majority of your money?
- What motivates you to be your best?
- When was the last time you lost your temper? About what?
- What will you never give up on?
- When you look into the past, what do you miss the most?
- What is the most spontaneous thing you've ever done?

- What makes you uncomfortable?
- What worries you about the future?
- What life lessons did you have to experience firsthand before you fully understood them?
- Do you like the city or town you live in? Why or why not?
- What's the best part of being you?
- When you look back over the past month, what single moment stands out?
- What is your happiest memory?
- What is your saddest memory?
- What would you like to change about yourself?
- What's the best decision you've ever made?
- Right now, at this moment, what do you want most?
- What makes love last?
- What good comes from suffering?
- What's the most important lesson you've learned in the last year?
- What was your last major accomplishment?
- Through all of life's twists and turns who has been there for you?
- What or who has been distracting you?
- What are you uncertain about?

- What are you looking forward to in the upcoming week?
- Who is your mentor and what have you learned from them?
- What do you think about when you lie awake in bed?
- What's something most people don't know about you?
- When you have a random hour of free time, what do you usually do?
- What makes you weird?
- If you could relive yesterday what would you do differently?
- What do you do over and over again that you hate doing?
- What white lies do you often tell?
- What is the biggest change you have made in your life in the last year?
- Whose life have you had the greatest impact on?
- Who impresses you?
- What have you done that you are not proud of?
- When should you reveal a secret that you promised you wouldn't reveal? Have you ever had to?
- How would you spend your ideal day?
- What is the one primary quality you look for in a significant other?

- What is the best advice you have ever received?
- If you could live forever, would you want to? Why?
- If you had to be someone else for one day, who would you be and why?
- What positive changes have you made in your life recently?
- Who makes you feel good about yourself?
- Which one of your responsibilities do you wish you could get rid of?
- What's something you don't like to do that you are still really good at?
- What type of person angers you the most?
- What is missing in your life?
- What is your most striking physical attribute?
- What has fear of failure stopped you from doing?
- Who would you like to please the most?
- If you could go back in time and change things, what would you change?
- When you meet someone for the very first time what do you want them to think about you?
- Who would you like to forgive?
- At what point during the last five years have you felt lost and alone?

- What is one opportunity you believe you missed out on when you were younger?
- What do you want more of in your life?
- What do you want less of in your life?
- Who depends on you?
- Who do you depend on?
- Who has had the greatest impact on your life?
- Are you happy with where you are in your life? Why?
- In one year from today, how do you think your life will be different?
- How have you sabotaged yourself in your life?
- Whom do you secretly envy? Why?
- What are you most excited about in your life right now ?
- What experience from this past year do you appreciate the most?
- How many hours of television do you watch in a week? A month? A year?
- What is the biggest obstacle that stands in your way right now?
- What do you sometimes pretend you understand that you really don't?
- What's something new you recently learned about yourself?

- What was the most defining moment in your life?
- What makes you feel secure?
- What are the top three qualities you look for in a friend?
- What simple gesture have you recently witnessed that renewed your hope in humanity?
- What recent memory makes you smile the most?
- What celebrities do you admire? Why?
- What is the number one motivator in your life right now?
- What music do you listen to to lift your spirits when you're feeling down?
- If I gave you $1000 and told you that you had to spend it today, what would you buy?
- What was the last thing that made you laugh out loud?
- Who was the last person you said "I love you" to?
- What is your biggest phobia?
- What are some recent compliments you've received?
- How much money per month is enough for you to live comfortably?
- When was your first impression of someone totally wrong?
- What do you love to do?

- What specific character trait do you want to be known for?
- Are you more like your mom or your dad? In what way?
- What is the number one quality that makes someone a good leader?
- What bad habits do you want to break?
- What is your favorite place on Earth?
- What questions do you often ask yourself?
- What are you an expert at?
- What things in life should always be free?
- What is something you have always wanted since you were a kid?
- What is the most recent dream you remember having while sleeping?
- What confuses you?
- In what way are you your own worst enemy?
- When did you not speak up when you should have?
- Where or who do you turn to when you need good advice?
- What artistic medium do you use to express yourself?
- Who or what is the greatest enemy of mankind?
- What's something you wish you had done earlier in life?

- What is the closest you have ever come to fearing for your life?
- How do you deal with isolation and loneliness?
- What do you know well enough to teach to others?
- What's a quick decision you once made that changed your life?
- What have you lost interest in recently?
- What makes life easier?
- What was the last thing you furiously argued about with someone?
- What is the number one solution to healing the world?
- What could society do without?
- What stresses you out?
- Where do you spend most of your time while you're awake?
- What makes someone a hero?
- When in your life have you been a victim of stereotyping?
- When was the last time you felt lucky?
- When did you first realize that life is short?
- What is the most insensitive thing a person can do?
- What can someone do to grab your attention?
- What's one downside of the modern day world?

- What simple fact do you wish more people understood?
- If you could do it all over again, would you change anything?
- Do you feel like you've lived this same day many times before?
- Are you living the life of your dreams?
- What would you do if fear was not a factor and you could not fail?
- What were you doing when you felt most passionate and alive?
- What are you most grateful for?
- What causes you stress in your life?
- Are you truly proud of the person that you are?
- Are there any toxic relationships in your life that need to be dealt with?
- Are you too hard on yourself or not hard enough?
- What worries you the most about your future?
- What dreams have you given up on?
- What do you need to change about yourself?
- What do you want to be remembered for at the end of your life?
- What makes you happy?

- Are you a good friend?
- Who would you trust with your life?
- What are you most afraid of?
- Are you a good communicator?
- Who are you most jealous of and why?
- Who are you?
- How would you describe yourself?
- What are you passionate about?
- What personal achievements are you most proud of?
- What are you most grateful for?
- What are the most important things to you in life?
- What do you represent?
- What do you want to embody?
- Do you love yourself? Why or why not?
- What do you love most about yourself?
- How can you love yourself more today?
- What is your ideal self?
- Look at your life now. Are you living the life of your dreams? Why or why not?
- If you have one year left to live, what would you do?
- If you have one week left to live, what would you do?
- If you have one day left to live, what would you do?
- What would you do today if there were no tomorrow?

- What are the biggest things you've learned in life to date?
- What advice would you give to your younger self?
- As your future self what advice would you give to your present self?
- Is there something you're still holding on to? Is it time to let it go?
- What opportunities are you looking for now? How can you create these opportunities?
- What are your biggest goals and dreams? Is there anything stopping you from pursuing them? Why? How can you address these factors?
- If you were to do something for free for the rest of your life, what would you want to do?
- What would you do if you cannot fail; if there were no limitations in money, resources, time, or networks?
- Are you putting any parts of your life on hold? Why?
- What's the top priority in your life right now? What are you doing about it?
- If you were to die tomorrow, what would be your biggest regret? What can you do now to make sure that it doesn't happen?
- What is your biggest frustration right now? What can you do about it?

- Looking back on your life, have you made any mistakes before? What happened, and why? What have you learned from those episodes?
- What is the biggest thing you can do now, that will change your life for the better? How can you start working on that?
- If you had a million dollars, what would you do with it?
- What is your ideal diet?
- What is your ideal home like?
- What is your ideal life?
- What do you fear most in life? Why?
- Is there anything you are running away from?
- Are you settling for less than what you are worth? Why?
- What is your inner dialogue like?
- What limiting beliefs are you holding on to?
- What bad habits do you want to break?
- What good habits do you want to cultivate?
- Where are you living right now — in the past, future, or present?
- Are you living your life to the fullest right now?
- What is the meaning of life?

- If you could have an adventure and be guaranteed not to get hurt, what would you do?
- If you had unlimited finances how would your life change?
- If you could, what one characteristic of your personality would you change? Why?
- Explained the ways you have earned money throughout your life.
- How would you describe the difference between a want and a need?
- What was the oddest gift you ever given or received?
- What natural talent do you wish you had?
- How do others react to your presence?
- What have others told you about yourself?
- What are your negative impressions of yourself?
- What are your positive impressions of yourself?
- Which politicians do you admire the most? Why?
- Which politicians do you admire the least? Why?
- Have you been a victim of harassment or discrimination because of your sexual orientation or gender identity?
- What life lesson gave you the most wisdom?
- What life lessons have you learned?

- What is your life purpose? Why do you exist? What is your mission?
- What drives you?
- What are the times you are most inspired, most motivated, most charged up?
- How can you change someone's life for the better today?
- Who inspire you the most? What can you do to be like them?
- Who is/are the most important person(s) to you in the world? Are you giving them the attention you want to give?
- Who are your mentors in life? (formal or informal)
- What is your definition of success?
- What are some of your wildest dreams and fantasies?
- What are some achievements that you wanted to make, but have not?
- Have you ever experienced legal issues? What were they?
- Have you ever seen something you can't explain?
- How should a person prepare for old age?

- Are you health conscious?
- Do you have any pet peeves?
- Have your ever disliked something and then changed your mind?
- Do you sing in the shower?
- What gives your life meaning?
- Are you happy with yourself?
- What makes you proud?
- Do you believe in ESP?
- What's the best part of growing older?
- What do you do to relieve stress?
- Are you in control of your life?
- Do you have any skeletons in your closet?

Tough Topics

Addictions and Substance Abuse

- Did you struggle with an addiction?
- What was the substance you were addicted to?
- How did the exposure to the substance begin?
- How and when did you realize that your use of the substance had developed into an addiction?
- What steps did you take to get help from this addiction?
- Were there any consequences that occurred from this addiction?
- Did someone you love struggle with an addiction?

Divorce

- Did your parents get a divorce?
- Have you gotten a divorce?
- How did your life change after your divorce?
- Did you have a support system during this time?
- What were the hardships for you after your divorce?
- What were the benefits from the divorce?
- What did you learn from the experience?
- Have you considered divorce, but never gone through with it? Share your thoughts about this.
- How have your beliefs changed about divorce?

Death

- Explain the experiences you have had with death.
- Explain your attitude regarding death.
- How have you handled your experiences with death?
- What advice do you have for dealing with death?
- Do you have fears about death?
- Do you have a will? Where is it located?
- What preparations have you taken for when you pass away?
- Do you believe you have had past lives? Do you have any memories from any of them?
- Have you written your obituary?

Some of Your Favorite Things

- What is your favorite song and why?
- What is your favorite quote?
- What is your favorite time of the year?
- What is your favorite fictional story? (novel, movie, fairytale, etc.)
- What's your favorite quote from a TV show/movie/book?
- Which meal is your favorite: breakfast, lunch, or dinner?
- What's your favorite season and why?
- What's your favorite board game?
- What's your favorite way to spend a day off?
- What type of music do you enjoy?
- What's your favorite ice cream topping?
- Dogs or Cats?
- Did you have a favorite pet?
- What was your favorite vacation? Where did you go and why was it special?
- What are your family's favorite jokes or pranks?
- What's your favorite book and why?
- What's your favorite movie and why?
- Who is your favorite historical figure?

- Do you have a favorite line in a piece of literature? A poem? Why do you relate to it?
- Where is your favorite place in the entire world to go?
- What are your top five favorite movies?
- What are some of your favorite songs?
- What is your favorite sound?
- What is your favorite smell?
- What's your favorite hobby to do alone?
- What is your favorite animal?
- Who is your favorite artist?
- Who is your favorite author?
- Who is your favorite actor?
- Who is your favorite musician?
- What is your favorite myth?
- What is your favorite season?
- What is your favorite time of day?
- What is your favorite flower?
- What is your favorite flavor of ice cream?
- What is your favorite Holiday?
- What is your favorite flower?
- What is your favorite bedtime story?
- What is your favorite bird?
- What is your favorite candy?

- What is your favorite car?
- What is your favorite city?
- What is your favorite color?
- What is your favorite dessert?
- What is your favorite drink?
- What is your favorite hobby?
- Who was your favorite teacher and why?
- What are some of your favorite recipes?

What Now?

Now that you've had time to go through this book, it might be time to think about the next steps. If you took the time to type out the answers to the questions you want to share with your family and friends now is a good time to think about how you want the finished product to look.

You can print off the responses, email them, create a shared document online, or you can turn all of your hard work into a book!

If you would like help turning your memories into something you can hold onto and flip through the pages, but aren't sure how to do it, I can help!

Go to **www.jessicaaikenhall.com/tellyourstory** to find out how!

If you're looking to share your story with friends and family, or are ready to share with a wider audience there is an option that will work for your needs.

Notes

Notes

Notes

Notes

Notes

Notes

Notes

Notes

Notes

Notes

Made in the USA
Columbia, SC
27 May 2022